Psil Silva's Psychedelic Crossword

Some are easy,
Some are hard.
Some may feel like the longest yard.

But keep on going,
Do not stop.
One day you will reach the top.

And when you're there,
Look out below.
Give a hand to friend or foe.

Help them up,
And you will find,
That it was you,
The entire time.

Tic-Tac-Toe

Psychedelic Drugs

Across

1 Doors of Perception

3 Quick trip!

4 Drug addiction

6 Cactus

7 Fungi

8 Special K

9 The Purge

Down

1 Found at your local home depot

2 Hofmann

5 Party drug

Famous Psychedelic Explorers

Across

3 LSD
5 If money were no object
6 Beat Poet
7 Be Here Now
8 Food of the Gods
9 Psychedelic Research Participant, writer, psychologist
10 Czech psychiatrist
11 Merry Pranksters

Down

1 Turn on, tune in, drop out
2 Beat Generation writer
4 Gonzo

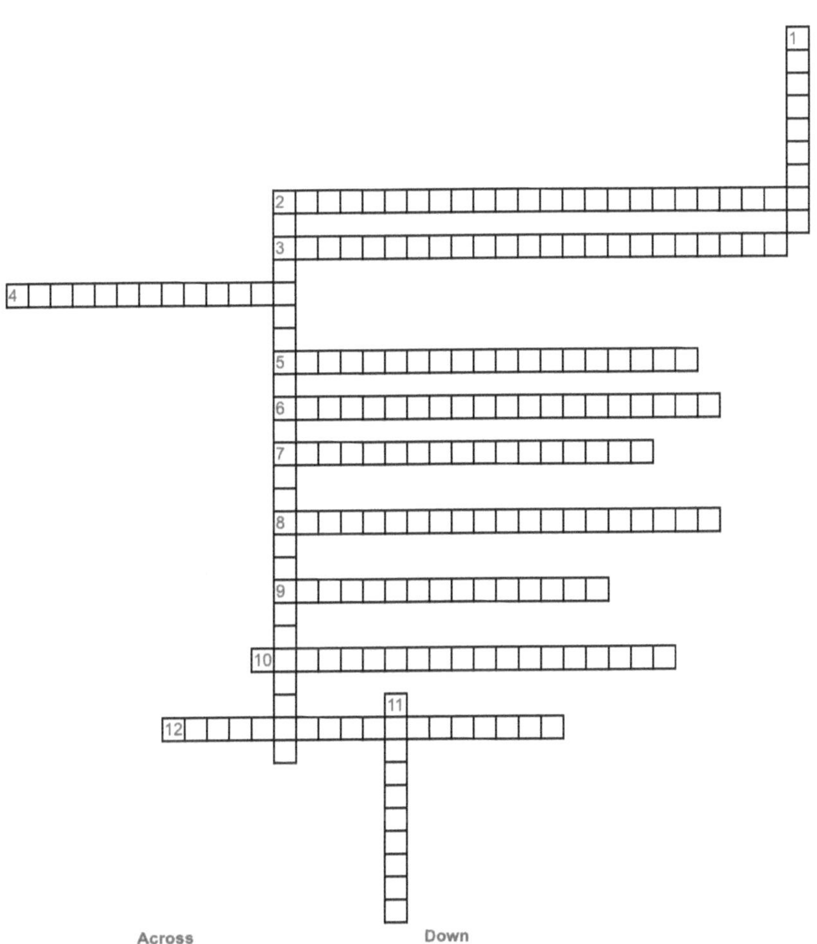

Across

2 A Manual…
3 The....In a colorfully painted bus
4 Journeying Amazon
5 New Science of Psychedelics
6 Rick Strassman Explores
7 Synthesize it
8 Explaining Mescaline
9 Sacred significance
10 Leary's phrase
12 Terence Adventures

Down

1 Psychedelics and Buddhism
2 Psil Silva's first
11 Leary's Adventures

Modern-Day Psychonauts

Across

2 Heffter Research
3 MAPS
4 Author, he might change your mind
5 Professional Mycologist
6 Up and coming, The Psychedelic Trip Journal
7 LSD doctor
8 Waking Up
9 The 4 hour man

Down

1 You've heard his podcast
2 There's a hyphen

Mostly Old-School Type Bands

Across

3 Isn't Life Strange
4 Sgt. Pepper
5 Are they really talkin' bout my generation?
6 Dark Side of the Moon
7 Not alive, but thankful
8 California Girls
9 Open and close these to get in places

Down

1 You Enjoy Myself
2 Time To Pretend
3 Sympathy For The Devil

Alice in Wonderland Characters

Across

- 3 Tea-time companion
- 4 # __ playing-card gardener
- 5 More pepper please
- 8 First Wonderland creature Alice encounters
- 10 Wonderland co-ruler
- 11 Hookah
- 12 Wonderland ruler
- 13 Meow
- 14 He likes his hats
- 15 Leads Alice to Wonderland
- 17 # __ playing-card gardener

Down

- 1 Cousin of the Queen
- 2 Alice's pet cat
- 3 Head of a calf
- 6 Leads Alice to Mock Turtle
- 7 Sleepy tea-time companion
- 9 # __ playing-card gardener
- 10 Quit stealin' them tarts!
- 16 How did I get here?

Psychedelic-Type Cartoons

Across

1 Blue jay, raccoon, and more
2 Sociopathic Chihuahua & friend
3 Ooo
4 Crazy genius scientist
5 Warner Bros.
6 Australian Wallaby
7 Surrealism in the silent film era

Down

1 Universe simulator

Psychedelic-Type Movies & Shows

Across

2 Programmer wins a contest
3 Dream within a dream
4 A pill changes everything
6 Modern day Twilight Zone
9 Virtual Reality
10 Johnny Depp A.I.

Down

1 Inspired by the Beatles
5 Transport anywhere
7 I'm blue dabadee dabadaa
8 Time-travel on the black market

Psytrance

Across

2   Simon Posford
4   DJ Lestat
6   Power Trance
8   If you take this much acid you might turn into a glass of orange juice
9   Wall outlets are filled with this, plus the cosmos
10   Don't eat too many of these or you'll get sick
12   Spongebob is a close relative

Down

1   I came I saw I conquered, almost
3   Do this with your eyes closed
5   Melodrama
7   Something on the keyboard
11   Asher Swissa and Assaf Bivas

Now & Then Psychedelic Artists

Across

1. Apprenticed with Fuchs in Austria
4. Their first name is a type of phone
5. Abstract Florescent Artist
6. Digital Artist. Full Sail.
7. The Daily & Max Studio
8. His life was a big psychedelic trip. He also cut off his ear
10. Peruvian-Canadian

Down

2. Mouse
3. Simon
9. Hyperspatial Reality

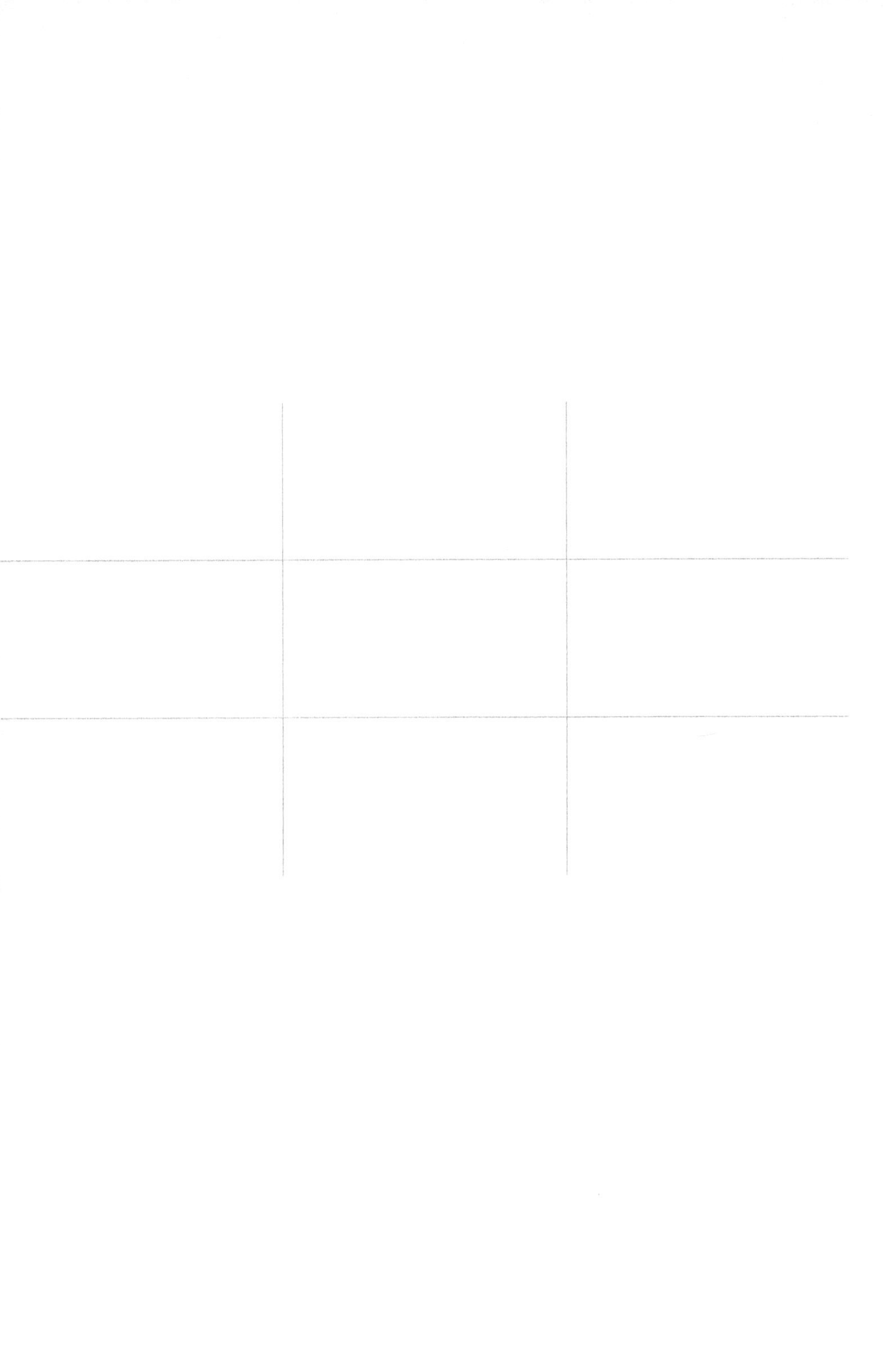

www.ingramcontent.com/pod-product-compliance
Lightning Source LLC
Chambersburg PA
CBHW051145250726
48655CB00007B/3256